THE LITTLE BOOK OF

Wellbeing

THE LITTLE BOOK OF

Wellbeing

60 ways to look good and feel great

Nikki Page

CICO BOOKS
LONDON NEW YORK

For my mother

Published in 2012 by CICO Books
an imprint of Ryland Peters & Small Ltd

20–21 Jockey's Fields, London WC1R 4BW
519 Broadway, 5th Floor
New York, NY 10012

www.cicobooks.com

1 3 5 7 9 10 8 6 4 2

A CIP catalog record for this book is available from the Library of Congress and the British Library.

ISBN: 978 1 908862 01 3

Printed in China

Editor: Marion Paull
Designer: Ian Midson
Cico photography: Emma Mitchell

For digital editions, visit www.cicobooks.com/apps.php

CICO BOOKS
LONDON NEW YORK

Contents

Foreword

I first met Nikki in the early 1990s and was immediately captivated by her extraordinary vibrancy and warmth. I imagined she was a couple of years older than I am, so was amazed when I discovered the gap was closer to 17 years—and she seems to have been getting younger ever since. However, Nikki does not have the weird jeunesse of a Hollywood star with a surgery habit, she has the true radiance that comes from a life well lived.

What swiftly becomes clear to everyone who knows her is that Nikki's vitality resonates from a deep level. She may be blessed with good looks, but the glow from within is what makes her so compelling. When she was in her twenties, Nikki suffered a near-fatal reaction to antibiotics, and after that devised an innovative approach to protecting her health that has paid dividends in the decades that have followed. I long ago decided that I would appoint Nikki as my health, beauty, and spirituality guru in the hope that some of her verve would rub off on me. In fact, I felt rather like the woman in "When Harry Met Sally," who looks at Meg Ryan simulating ecstasy in a café and declares, "I'll have what she's having."

Nikki took me under her wing and I soon discovered that the Page approach to wellbeing included large doses of vitamin C, regular yoga, learning to breathe properly, positive thinking, a healthy diet, herbal tea, a spot of sun (but don't forget the sun cream,) brisk walks, spiritual nourishment, and, ideally, the companionship of a four-pawed friend. She bolstered my confidence and my professional ambitions, and she even gave me an excellent tip on "how to make your boyfriend propose to you." (He did, and I look forward to that particular tip being in her next book!)

You will have heard some of her advice elsewhere, but never so well integrated; or presented in a way that is so easy to adopt. Nikki will not enjoin you to spend hours at a gym, to make your own face cream, or to eat only macrobiotic food. She understands that in our frantic, time-poor world people need simple, clear ways to reinvigorate themselves. I love the fact that Nikki's exercise regime is so realistic: she does 15 minutes of yoga a day and takes a walk whenever she can, even if it's just to the post office. That's it, yet at the age of 60 she's the most supple, youthful, and energetic person I know.

My favorite chapter of the book is the "mind & spirit" section, because Nikki is so wise about family, friends, love, and the importance of joy and the tonic of laughter. She also makes the vital point that it's near impossible to achieve personal gains without learning to give. So much health and beauty advice nowadays seems centered on the cult of self, but Nikki's philosophy is based on reaching out to others.

I have known Nikki in many incarnations: as a local politician, a candidate for London mayor, a home renovator, a charity fundraiser, a fashion designer's muse, a dance-floor queen, and as the best friend any woman could ever ask for. She has been impressive in all of them, but I firmly believe her most inspiring role will be as Vitality Tsar.

Rowan Pelling

Rowan Pelling is a *Daily Telegraph* columnist, a *Daily Mail* agony aunt, writer, and broadcaster.

My story

I have never believed in being half-hearted. As the old adage goes, if it's worth doing, it's worth doing with gusto! So when I shimmied onto a catwalk aged 16, I had already spent three months doing a proper modeling course—even though modeling was just supposed to be a way to help me earn some cash when I was at college studying to be a fashion buyer.

I never completed that college course. A modeling agent spotted me at a university fashion show and I headed for London. I thought I'd made the big time, but as I discovered, there was almost always someone prettier, cleverer, funnier, more glamorous, and more capable than me. It was an important first lesson: don't mind when others are better, just

learn from them. I learned how to look confident even if my knees were knocking and how to look my best: walking tall, sitting elegantly, entering a room looking like you own it. Knowing how to walk upstairs or get into a car are all very easy things to do well. Understanding what suits you and feeling good about how you look makes you look self-assured, which is one of the keys to success.

As with the modeling, virtually everything in my working life came about through opportunity rather than planning. I was the beneficiary of many changes that started in the sixties, which encouraged companies to give women a shot at different types of work even though they may not have had the perfect qualifications for the job. Despite having a relatively limited education, I became a successful marketing executive with Visa International and Intercontinental Hotels, and consultant to a variety of companies with different interests. In 1994, I found myself elected as Westminster Councillor in London, where I chaired first the Environment Committee and then Housing. In 2002, I sought the Conservative party's nomination for London Mayor. I poured my heart into politics and into voluntary work, and more recently into working for Variety, the children's charity.

This was achieved despite being chronically sick for most of my life following an acute illness, which I contracted aged 20 (more of that later). Finding ways to carry on and join in everyday life led me to have a passion for healthy living and to develop a lifestyle that allowed me to live normally. I never lost my interest in looking good and my belief that confidence opens doors.

I have written a 10-minute yoga column for the *Daily Telegraph* and contribute to their health section from time to time. Not long ago, I wrote about the extraordinary effect a visit to herbalist Susan Koten had on my wellbeing. Both Susan and I were astounded at how the piece struck a chord with so many people. I realized then that thousands and thousands of people are struggling through life feeling tired, lethargic, and off-color, and not knowing which way to turn. Recently, I turned 60 and started the year feeling very apprehensive about reaching my sixth decade, but something happened: as I confided in friends and associates how miserable I was at the thought, they overwhelmed me with their generosity about how I looked and how young they thought I seemed. I am fortunate to have many younger friends and they, in particular, demanded to know my secrets. And so I realized that my drive for a healthy life had the added benefit of making me look, as well as feel, better.

That's how the idea for this book was born—but it could all have been a very different story.

Aged 20, I nearly died from antibiotic poisoning from Septrin, which had been given to me for a stomach infection. It is now known to be a high-risk antibiotic but in those days it was the new wonder drug. My parents were summoned back from vacation and, together with my brother and sister-in-law, called to my bedside in hospital. My eyes and nails bled. I was ulcerated inside and out and I was blind for days. I looked so dreadful that the nurses wouldn't let me near a mirror for two weeks. Once released from hospital, aftercare included being told "not to go anywhere in public for six months": if I caught an infection, they didn't think they could treat it. That was it. There was no guidance or advice on how to deal with the aftermath or what to expect. To be fair, I don't think anyone knew. No one suggested that since my entire stomach had been ulcerated and damaged by the drugs, I could have serious problems with digestion, absorbing nutrients, and with certain types of foods. For years I struggled against a range of debilitating side effects and lost faith in most of the medical profession.

At that time, alternative remedies and complementary medicine were treated with great suspicion and were not readily available. I was determined to feel well again and tried a host of expensive and different alternative remedies. Many helped in the short term but it took decades of trial and error to find a way to achieve sustainable energy and fitness levels. During this time, I learned how to keep going, appear normal, hold down exacting jobs, and enjoy some kind of social life. I developed ways to cope— finding quiet places to sit and breathe so that I was ready for the next meeting; never showing how ill I often felt; carrying food with me so that I could slip out for a snack rather than have people think I was a faddish eater.

Close friends knew my history and were incredibly kind and, as I grew older, I became much bolder in saying why I had to watch my diet so carefully. It seemed better than having people think I had some sort of weird diet fetish!

I have learned that there are many, many people who for all sorts of reasons feel ill and are unhappy because they don't know how to make themselves feel better. It has made me passionate about promoting a lifestyle that allows anyone to look and feel great.

I have also learned that respecting and valuing the whole food chain is very important. I loathe any form of waste or cruelty to animals and care deeply about the environment.

I am not a nutritionist, a yoga teacher, or a scientist. This little book is about my own 40-year journey to wellbeing. My hope is that it may inspire and work for you, too!

A word about aging

Aging is not fun. That is not to say there are no advantages to being older but in my experience they have little to do with how you look. Aging means the body is slowing up; it means creaky joints, less flexibility, and the gradual thickening of waist and thighs. Then there's the unnerving realization that you almost never leave home without having to go back for something you've forgotten! Reaching each decade has a particular effect on our psyche. I really didn't mind being 30. I wasn't thrilled about 40, was distinctly less than excited about 50, and was positively horrified at the thought of turning 60. After all, you don't actually feel any different inside. There's still a fit, vibrant woman in there, yearning to do all the things she's always loved, and she wants to look and feel as attractive as she possibly can.

To look as good as you can means making choices and it's never to late to start. Most of what I do is common sense but it has to be a life choice. It's the regularity that makes the difference. When you choose the healthy path, a better future awaits; more energy, fitness, alertness, and a feeling of achievement in being the best that you can—all of which gives you more confidence.

This little book is divided into three parts, which, for me, has made for a happier, fitter life. I hope you find in it an easy way to enhance yours.

The good news is that once you make that choice and it becomes how you live, there is very little desire left for a less healthy way of living

PART 1

Looking Good

Whatever we want from life, confidence plays a major part in succeeding. I have blessed my mother a thousand times for encouraging me to go to modeling school when I was in my teens. It doesn't matter whether or not you have the looks to be a supermodel. What matters is that you look confident, the best you can, and that you know how to appear in control most of the time. I relished everything I was taught and still practice most of the techniques I learned: how to climb stairs, enter a room, get in and out of a car, sit elegantly, and walk tall. I am sure that I would never have achieved the same in business without that training.

1 practice yoga

Yoga is about helping to maintain a healthy body and mind

Yoga is a gentle form of exercise that allows you to stretch out your spine and keep supple at any age. The breathing techniques help to reduce stress and instil a sense of wellbeing. One of the best things about yoga, particularly if you practice it in the privacy of your own home, is that you do it at entirely your own pace. Your stretches should be what is comfortable for you. Yoga is not about competition!

I have always led a very busy and often unpredictable life, so regular yoga classes were not really an option for me; nor was I able to do much in the way of aerobic exercise following my illness. However, I taught myself yoga over 30 years ago (with occasional visits to a professional to check my technique.) I have made it part of my daily routine ever since and would no more start the day without practicing yoga than forgo brushing my teeth.

My daily practice takes 10 to 15 minutes and I really stretch my body, toning every part and keeping remarkably flexible. I once stopped for a couple of months and put two inches on my waist and the top of my hips! I make sure my spine is properly stretched, which helps battle natural height loss and the facial exercises help keep the face and neck muscles tighter.

2 perfect your posture

If you look confident, you start to feel it

Nothing ages a person more quickly than bad posture. I come from an era when we were taught to walk with books on our heads and were awarded stripes at school if we had good deportment. Good posture stretches the spine, improves digestive function, and boosts confidence. In my first job I learned the basics of feeling and looking good. Modeling was one of the most useful courses I've ever done because, even if I'm feeling nervous, I can walk into a room looking confident. What's more, if you look confident, people react more positively to you.

look and feel fabulous

❋ Walk tall: position your hips slightly forward, imagine an invisible thread from the top of your head to the sky, tuck your chin in, and relax those shoulders. You are positively gliding and already look five years younger!

❋ Ensure your desk chair is the correct height. Use a cushion if it is too low, so you can sit with your back straight. This also improves digestion and breathing.

❋ To get in a car, keep your legs together and put your bottom on the seat first. That way you're not bending your spine, you're using your stomach muscles, and it looks so much more elegant! The same when you get out—feet first, together, and hold the door as you stretch the body and use your stomach muscles to straighten up.

3 breathe properly

If you don't breathe properly, your body can't function properly

The importance of breathing properly is mentioned in each section of this book. The breathing part of yoga is almost as important as the stretching, and if you combine the two, you will find your body unwinds and stretches out. It's a wonderfully liberating feeling. Before starting your exercises, take deep breaths right down into your abdomen. When practicing yoga, as a general rule, breathe in as you take a position and exhale as you release it. If in doubt, just breathe deeply during exercises. The most important factor is to ensure that fresh oxygen is circulating through your whole body (for a simple breathing exercise, see page 84.)

4 walk, walk, walk!

Arguments rage about what sort of exercise is really good for you, and what can adversely affect your joints, and then there's the time and expense factor of gyms and other sporting pastimes to consider. The easy thing to do is to walk everywhere that you possibly can—even manufacture reasons to walk places. Invest in a pair of decent trainers and carry your pretty shoes in your bag to be worn when you reach your destination. Walk with strides as long and easy as are comfortable, at a decent speed, head attached to the sky and bottom firmly clenched. Your thighs and bottom will be firmer, you'll feel fitter, and your stomach will be tighter. It's also an ideal time to be in a quiet place with your thoughts and aspirations.

how to walk more:

Allow extra time to get wherever you're going, and get off the bus or subway at an earlier stop, or park the car a little farther away. Always walk up escalators, never stand.

I actively encourage myself to go out by making lists of things I need from the store. I try to get out at least twice a day to run errands.

When I'm writing, I schedule "walking breaks" and take myself off for 10 or 15 minutes. Even if it's only around the block, it's good exercise and helps keep the body moving.

5 keep your skin clean and soft

Every part of your body needs attention

Cleanse and moisturize your face twice daily. Your skin can't absorb cream if it's dirty. Those pores need to be kept clean and refined. My mother bought me a pot of cold cream and some pure rose water when I was 13 as I have typically English fair skin and she thought soapy water would be too harsh on it. I have cleansed and toned twice each day ever since. Use a simple, pure moisturizer that suits your own skin tone. I tend to favor small suppliers who make their own mostly organic products. I enjoy supporting cottage industries and particularly love the purity of the products. Check out if there's someone near you who is making some gorgeous cream that is relatively inexpensive and pure. Look out for organic baby balm products in your local grocery store or pharmacist—they may be meant for babies' bottoms but can work wonders on your face, too!

Moisturize your body every day after your bath or shower. Every part of your body needs attention and constant moisturizing really helps. Look for big pots of moisturizer in the sales, but you need to check the labels. I always try to stay away from anything with too many ingredients, especially parabens. These are chemicals used as preservatives in cosmetics, and even some foods.

using natural products is important:

Whatever you put on your body is absorbed into it. The purer the products, the fewer chemicals you're putting into your body.

Buying organic products encourages more organic farming, and so helps to keep the countryside and wildlife freer from unnecessary pesticides.

Supporting local businesses that are in turn supporting the local environment and economy is good for everyone!

6 exfoliate

Exfoliation is an easy way to help keep your skin younger looking

It's not enough just to moisturize your body. You need to give your skin a proper spring clean regularly, sloughing off all those nasty dead cells. As your skin regenerates, so the dead cells stay attached to your body. These cause it to feel a bit uneven, and prevent moisturizer from being properly absorbed. The process of exfoliation also helps to increase circulation.

Treat yourself to a loofah or exfoliating cloth. Rub in your exfoliator cream, paste, or lotion thoroughly before getting into the bath or shower. Then take it off with firm strokes, always working from the outer edges of your body in toward the heart. Do it at least once a month but more if you can. Sugar body scrubs are less abrasive on the skin than salt ones.

The face needs exfoliation, too. A gentle exfoliation of the face every week is a very good way to keep the skin soft and help stimulate your natural collagen production. Collagen is that magic ingredient in your skin that regenerates it, making it look and feel younger. As you age, it works less effectively, which is one of the principal reasons our skin starts to sag and wrinkle. If done regularly, exfoliation is an easy way to help keep your skin younger looking. Be sure to use a product designed for the face that is not too abrasive.

7 teeth

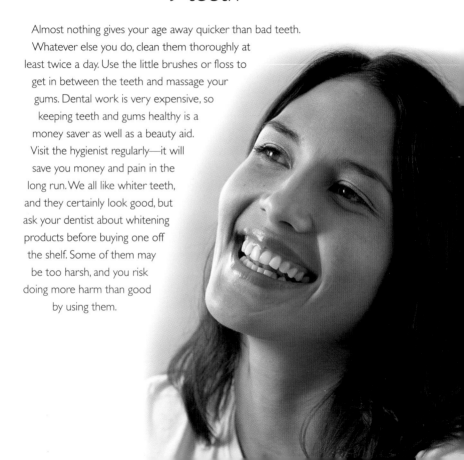

Almost nothing gives your age away quicker than bad teeth. Whatever else you do, clean them thoroughly at least twice a day. Use the little brushes or floss to get in between the teeth and massage your gums. Dental work is very expensive, so keeping teeth and gums healthy is a money saver as well as a beauty aid. Visit the hygienist regularly—it will save you money and pain in the long run. We all like whiter teeth, and they certainly look good, but ask your dentist about whitening products before buying one off the shelf. Some of them may be too harsh, and you risk doing more harm than good by using them.

8 young hands and nails

If you can, have regular manicures

Keeping your hands and nails looking good makes a big difference to how old you look overall. Keep pots of moisturizer or handcream by every sink, by your bed, and by your favorite chair where you sit to watch TV. Make it a habit to apply handcream every time you wash up, sit down, and especially before you go to sleep. I always rub pure vitamin E oil onto my hands just before I switch out the light. If your nails are discolored or flaky, see a good nutritionist or herbalist to see if you need to adjust your diet or take some supplements. If you're not sure which nutrients you need, have a chat with someone at your local health store or take a look at Hazel Courteney's *500 of the Most Important Health Tips You'll Ever Need.* It's my personal bible!

9 fabulous feet

I have failed miserably with my own feet so this advice is for those of you who are younger and still have a chance to save yours! I lived in high heels and pointed toes from my teens right through to my fifties—the result is bunions and discomfort. I am not proud of my feet. Now I wear high heels just when I go out and always have a pair of flat shoes in my bag or car. Regular pedicures are good and make you feel terrific but nothing works as well as wearing footwear that actually fits you most of your life!

Recently, I had surgery on my right foot to replace an arthritic joint with a titanium one. It's certainly worked for me! Now I have one straight foot and I don't seem to set off the alarm systems at airports, either! If, like me, you've already wrecked your feet, check out having bunions removed or toe joints replaced.

10 take care of your hair
Don't overwash and blow dry your hair

Trim your hair regularly, and use natural hair products so that your scalp doesn't dry out. It is important to read labels. Health stores will have shampoos made from natural ingredients, and several leading brands make organic shampoos.

If your hair starts to thin, see a specialist and/or a herbalist or nutritionist. My own hair is naturally very frizzy. I have spent half my life with a large hairbrush in one hand and a hairdryer in the other. Dampness in the air was always a nightmare, and vacations a challenge of epic proportions! Now I have a Brazilian blow dry which is a real lifesaver. This fabulous new treatment is available at most hairdressers. The hair is coated in keratin, making it much more manageable and preventing the dreaded frizz. Different types of treatment suit different types of hair, though, so make sure you use a product that's right for you. And be warned—when it's first applied, you have to leave it on for three days, so you'll need to pick a suitable time.

Try not to overbleach your hair, and use only natural coloring products. I have very fine streaks in my hair, which I replenish about twice a year. If you have some gray, it's a good tip to make sure it blends in with your color, so that no starkly different-colored roots show as your hair grows. That keeps a natural look for longer, and the fewer times you color your hair, the better it is—for your hair and your wallet. Also, don't overwash and blow dry your hair. The more you wash it, the more it needs it. I generally get by on a couple of times a week. Hair is, of course, affected by diet, and Hazel Courteney's fantastic book (see page 109) provides a list of beneficial nutrients and foods.

If your hair is dry, frizzy, sun-damaged, or color-damaged, if you have a flaky scalp, or even if your hair is just a bit tired and listless, try my favorite coconut oil treatment. It really works. Buy some pure coconut oil from a health store or supermarket. Gently melt the oil in a pan, then part your hair in several places as if you are going to color it, brush the oil along the partings, and massage it well into the scalp so your hair is sodden with it. Then leave it on for as long as you can. You can always put on a shower cap and sleep in it. I once slicked my coconutty hair into a tie at the back of my neck and left it on for 24 hours! The longer you leave it, the better the result. Wash it out with your regular shampoo. Your hair will feel thicker and more manageable, and your shoulders will be free of those pesky white flakes.

11 bright eyes

Eyes are the windows of the soul

Eyes are pretty much everyone's best feature. If you don't look after them, you will have terrible wrinkles as you age. Remove eye make-up with a proper remover, and gently massage them every time you moisturize your face to help stop puffiness and keep them clear. Lightly run the heels of your thumbs up the bridge of your nose, and press just under the inner end of each eyebrow. You'll feel when you have the right spot. Then tap around the eyes with your forefinger, under the brows and along the top of the cheekbone under the eye. Never put heavy oils or creams too close to the eye and never ever rub them or pull the skin about. Always have a light touch and work inward from the outer edge of the eye.

12 lovely lips

As we age, lips have a tendency to become thinner because our natural collagen is less effective. Thinner lips and fine lines around the mouth are key signs of aging. To help prevent that, and to maintain lips at their best, it is important to take special care of them. First of all, don't smoke—that will age your mouth quicker than anything else. When you exfoliate your face, make sure that you rub around the lips gently. Special lip exfoliators are available, if your budget will run to one. There are also lip-plumping creams. I always use one after brushing my teeth. You can, of course, have botox or filler in the lips, but do be careful—the result is not always a good look! And once you have a trout pout, there doesn't seem to be anything that you can do about it.

13 fabulous facials

A regular facial ensures your skin is super clean

Having a facial is a special treat. There are few things more relaxing and beneficial as a pick-me-up for the skin than a facial. All sorts of different types are available now. All the pores are thoroughly cleansed, blackheads removed, greasy spots reduced, dry patches rehydrated, skin tone evened out, and dead skin dislodged.

Looking after your skin by cleansing, moisturizing, and exfoliating properly makes a big difference, and it is so easy to apply a mask now and again. For a natural tightening mask, I whisk up an egg white (you can eat the yolk!) and lather it on my skin. One egg white will last for several applications so put it in a sealed container in the fridge and apply morning and night until it runs out. It really does make the skin feel firmer.

If you can, go to a professional. A trained therapist will help keep your skin looking good and will notice such things as age spots starting to develop. You may need to use a higher skin factor cream to help prevent the situation worsening. Try to have a facial at least twice a year.

14 bottom crunches

The easiest exercise of all! Just clench your bottom muscles, feeling them tighten, and then release. Angelina Jolie may have been born with a perfect bottom but most of us have to work at it! Actually, it's not just about the way our rears look!

I do at least 20 of these every morning before my yoga. I would like a perter bottom—mine is rather small and flat—but more importantly, it helps you keep control over the need to rush to the bathroom. As we age, these muscles need to be kept taut and this really does work. I also tend to do a few if I'm sitting in the car in a traffic jam, while I'm at my desk, or even sitting on the bus.

15 just enough sun

Our bodies need vitamin D and the best source
is natural sunlight

So much sensible advice is available about how to sunbathe safely and always using sunscreen. I have very fair skin that burns quickly so I have always been careful. My skin is remarkably undamaged by sun for my age, and it was worth lathering on the factor 30-plus for much of my life. I love lying in the sun but I also love reading a book in the shade, and I make sure I never get too hot.

However, I do not put a sunscreen on my face every day in the winter. I like to let it breathe a bit, and some sunshine on the skin will do more good than harm. Our bodies need vitamin D and the best source is natural sunlight so you will have to use your own judgment and notice how strong the sun is wherever you are. If it's a warm early spring day in Texas or England, you are unlikely to need a hat or sunscreen, but if you're in Florida or Rome at the same time, you may well need to put sunscreen on your face, and if you're in Hawaii or Singapore you will need both!

16 look after your back and joints

If your spine is not straight and supple, it is much harder for the rest of your body to function

I almost never have backache and I put that down to having practiced yoga for over 30 years and keeping my spine supple. I have had occasional problems with joints but for me those are cured by the right diet. I also take a good Omega 3 supplement every day.

If your spine is not straight, it is much harder for the rest of your body to function properly. You can't breathe or digest well if your spine is bent. If you don't breathe properly, it's harder to concentrate and remain relaxed. See page 21 for a simple yoga exercise that stretches the spine.

Diet is very important for healthy joints. Include plenty of fresh fruit and vegetables, and oily fish, such as mackerel or sardines, or take omega oil supplements. Body oils or creams containing natural omega-rich oil are good, too. Remember: what you massage onto your body goes into your body. If, like me, you're concerned about overfishing, many plant-based omega supplements are available from health-food stores.

If you suffer from joint pain, consult a qualified nutritionist or ask your doctor to test you for food intolerances or a lack of specific minerals and oils. If you have a tendency to arthritis, asthma, or eczema, you may wish to try removing gluten, oranges, milk, cheese, sugar, and chocolate from your diet.

17 enjoy massage and reflexology

Practitioners can feel where your body needs extra help and support and ease the tension

For me, massage and reflexology are among life's greatest luxuries. Regular massages help tone the skin and relax and de-stress the body. What's more, if blood flow is sluggish, or you are feeling under par, it may be that your lymphatic system is not functioning properly. This means that the waste materials in your whole system are not being eliminated efficiently. Massage and reflexology are ideal ways to improve lymphatic drainage.

If every health-insurance company and health service prescribed free massages and reflexology instead of medicines for stress, angst, and insomnia, I'm sure it would save a lot of money and patients would be much happier and healthier!

I have found reflexology—massaging pressure points on feet and hands—to be enormously beneficial. In many instances, a good reflexologist has been able to improve my symptoms of bloating and discomfort with a professional prod on my feet. Reflexology works by pressure being applied to certain points on your hands or, more usually, your feet, which connect with different parts of your body. Try to visit a reflexologist at least four times a year, and go to a registered practitioner. Reflexologists will often give you advice on where to apply pressure yourself for your own particular sensitivity.

Remember, it is important to drink plenty of water after a treatment to ensure that all those nasty chemicals and other poisons in your system are properly eliminated.

18 cold laser light treatment

Acupuncture stimulation without needles

This treatment delivers acupuncture stimulation without needles by using light instead. On the face, it can help get rid of acne, broken capillaries, open pores, eye bags, crow's feet, eczema, psoriasis, wrinkles, and fine lines. On the body, it helps break down fat cells and encourages lymphatic drainage.

Laser light treatment has been around for a while. However, a new machine, made by Lipogenie, is now operational, which uses three different levels of laser light in order to increase the skin's own collagen production. An amazing, very experienced therapist, Katherine Jackson (see page 108), and I have been experimenting with this. Katherine is one of the frontrunners in using this treatment. Just one session makes you look and feel good for a special night out but a series of them can really perk up the skin in the long term, although of course you need top-ups. Katherine uses the machine in conjunction with her own serum, made from all-natural glycans.

Glycans are thought to be the new super ingredient for promoting collagen production. In high-street brands, they are mostly synthetic but they do occur naturally in some varieties of seaweed. You may find that using a cream or serum containing glycans makes a real difference—especially if you start while you are still quite young.

I am really impressed by the results. Not only is my skin noticeably plumper but the little bags that were beginning to form under my eyes seem to have completely gone.

The company that makes the machines is better known for its medical work, but harnessing natural light to boost collagen production benefits those who just want to look good as well as those who have medical conditions requiring help with the skin. Katherine developed the serum herself and uses only natural products—there is no perfume, even natural, in any of her creams. She's very much a cottage industry but beauticians all around the world are now making beautiful pure lotions, much of it available on the internet, and therapists are available internationally.

19 spa days

Candles, aromas, and soft music ease away stress and strain

I am a total spa junkie. I love the fabulous feeling of peace and relaxation that wafts over you as you enter a spa. The candles, aromas, and soft music ease away stress and strain like nothing else. In most spas, you can soothe those tense shoulders under a jet of water before having a favorite treatment, and unwind in relaxation rooms. However, it is expensive. You could ask family and friends to club together for a birthday or Christmas treat, but if that's not an option, you can always create your very own special home experience.

First, make sure you have set aside proper "you" time: children, partners, flatmates, and anyone else must be banned for at least an hour. Turn off all your phones. Next create the space. It's hard to relax in a messy, cluttered room. I make a spa in my bathroom and relax in my bedroom afterward, so ensure both are clean and tidy. Then I set about the rituals of creating a beautiful, relaxing ambiance. Just going through the motions sends a signal to my subconscious that I'm about to relax. It's often the little touches that make professional spas so special and you create some of them at home. Prepare a pretty tray with a cloth and a few flowers or petals. Put some herbal tea in a flask to keep in warm and add some still mineral water and fresh fruit. The idea is to have everything ready before cocooning yourself.

making a lovely home spa experience:

Warmth—Ensure that your chosen rooms are cozy. If you're going to lie on your bed after a bath, make sure you can snuggle into a fresh blanket or clean sheets.

Scents—Light incense sticks and perfumed candles so that delicious smells waft everywhere. For a bath, treat yourself to some essential oil mixed into apricot kernel or other base oil. Ylang Ylang is one of my favorites, and jasmine and lavender are both fabulous. Experiment by mixing different oils together to make something that is perfect for you. Just a few drops turns a regular bath into a luxury.

Music—Choose something with waves and gentle sounds to help you waft into a dreamy place, or anything that is uplifting and gently relaxing.

If you have the time, slowly massage your whole body with a scented oil or cream after your bath, and do some long yoga stretches while your body is still warm and before wrapping up to rest. All these things add to your overall enjoyment, relaxation, and renewal.

20 confidence boosters
The way you hold yourself costs nothing

I talked earlier about the confidence that taking a modeling course in my teenage years has given me. Here are a few tips that I learned then. During my life, I've been both completely broke and quite comfortable financially. Whatever your circumstances, you can always look confident and in control. The way you hold yourself makes all the difference to how you feel and how other people perceive you.

Good posture

✳ Never ever slouch! Always walk tall. Sit and stand with your back straight.

✳ Before entering a room, consciously straighten your back, drop your shoulders, hold your head straight, and feel tall. Ensure that your dress/jacket/trousers are not tucked or crumpled anywhere. Place your hand on the door knob and open the door firmly but quite slowly—you don't want to knock anyone standing behind it—and step inside. If it's a party or gathering, linger for a moment or two, to spot someone you know, and walk purposefully over to them. If you don't know anyone, look for a place you can head for meaningfully. I sometimes go to exhibitions on my own and head for a painting with perhaps just one other person looking at it. That often opens the door for conversation. If you look friendly and confident, it's much easier to strike up conversations with people you don't know.

✳ Gauge how high or low a seat is before you go to sit down. There's nothing quite so unsettling as either hitting a high chair with a bump or disappearing into a soft sofa that is a foot lower than you anticipated. Rest a hand on an arm or table if you're worried about losing your balance, make sure your feet and legs are together, and lower yourself gently, bottom first.

✳ It is generally more elegant to go up and downstairs at a slight angle.

✳ When you arrive and go to take off your coat, always unbutton from the bottom upward. That way your coat sits properly until you take it off. Then gently shrug it off your shoulders. When putting it back on, someone may be helping you but if not, make sure you have your sleeves ready for your arms before setting about the process, and always fasten the top button first. It makes the coat hang well and also ensures you have the buttons done up in the right places. Little things like that avoid embarrassing moments.

PART 2
Staying Healthy

If you don't feel well and are constantly picking up minor infections, it's hard to look good or get the most out of life. There are many reasons why you may not be as well as you could be. Your diet may not be good for you; you may be taking too little exercise; you may be carrying too much weight; you may not be sleeping well—or all four. Bags under the eyes, bloated stomach, headaches, swollen fingers, or any number of minor symptoms may mean you are eating foods that don't suit you (see page 66.) Staying healthy should be a lifestyle choice, not an occasional fix. When you are in tune with your body, your energy soars and there are so many benefits, you really won't ever want to go back to your old ways.

21 say no to pharmaceuticals

The more you can avoid putting anything unnatural into your body, the better

Yes, I know we are endlessly told that these are safe, and that pesticides and chemicals are needed to produce enough food. Well, far be it from me to argue with the scientists, but I think there are way too many pharmaceuticals around, and the more you can avoid putting anything unnatural either into or on your body, the better.

If you have a headache, for example, the chances are you ate something that didn't agree with you, or you are stressed and need to soothe the muscles around the shoulders or head. If there's no one to give you a massage, you can ease some of the pressure points yourself, have a cup of relaxing herbal tea— there are loads to choose from—change what you're eating, and go for a walk in the fresh air. If you have regular aches, pains, or problems, check with a doctor and if it's nothing serious, consult a good nutritionist or herbalist, who may well be able to help you.

Masking pain and treating symptoms does not get to the root of a problem. Talk to practitioners who take a holistic view.

to ease pressure on tight muscles in the neck:

Take an empty paper-towel roll, or a posterboard roll that had gift wrap around it, and tap it firmly around your neck and on the top of your shoulders.

Gently massage your own shoulders using your three fore fingers to ease the muscles either side of your neck. Use your right hand to ease the tensions in your left shoulder and your left hand for the right shoulder.

Stand with your feet slightly apart and drop your body gently down from the waist, allowing your hands to fall freely in front of you until your palms are on the floor or you are stretched as far as is comfortable. Then very gently unfold your body, almost feeling each disc in your spine as you stand straight again. Put your arms behind your back and link your fingers together. Now hunch your shoulders forward and back to help release the tension in your shoulder muscles. Finally, keeping your fingers linked, straighten your arms and raise them away from your body. Then let your arms fall back by your sides and relax.

22 breathe properly

Look for something beautiful that nature has provided

Every part of your body needs oxygen to survive, so breathe deeply. Make sure you get as much fresh air as you can, and take time to feel your breathing. It's the most important thing you do! If you live in a busy town, seek out your nearest green space for a quick walk during the working day. It may be a leafy street or even a cemetery. It's important to be "present" when you go out for fresh air. That is to say, really look at your surroundings, notice any tree or flower. If it's a sunny day, look at the sky; if it's raining, think of the water washing away any stress you feel; if it's snowing, marvel at the snowflakes. Take some really deep breaths, from your stomach, allowing your body to relax and de-stress.

23 eat wholesome food

I eat as much organic food as I can. Despite conflicting studies about whether organic food is better than intensively produced varieties, I cannot help but believe that the purer the food you eat, the better it is for you. After all, if you were lucky enough to drive an Aston Martin, you wouldn't go down to the local supermarket to buy the least expensive oil possible to put in its engine, would you? Well, your body is an even more beautifully crafted machine than an Aston Martin, so why would you want to fill it with anything less than the best you can?

I care very much that the production of anything I consume has caused as little harm as possible to the environment, and has not damaged any natural habitat. I care about overfishing, and I want to know that any animal that has given its life to be my food has had a decent existence before being slaughtered. Yes, I know it is more expensive but I eat much less because of that, which has other benefits.

24 say no to recreational drugs

Never be tempted to take recreational drugs. You cannot be sure what's in them, they take you out of control of yourself, and they cannot possibly make you feel better in the long term or make you look better—just think of all those pictures of celebrities with collapsed noses! And don't smoke! It will make you smell awful, your mouth wrinkly and ugly, as well as possibly giving you mouth, throat, or lung cancer.

25 limit alcohol

If you're happy in yourself, you don't need a drink to relax

I used to love vodka and wine, and then I suddenly realized that it wasn't suiting me. I stopped drinking and initially felt slightly awkward when I seemed like a party pooper. Interestingly, very few of my friends drink much now and many have expressed pleasure at being able to go out with someone who doesn't want to drink much, either. I haven't drunk much for more than 15 years and feel so much better for it. There is so much evidence that alcohol is a contributory cause of various cancers, much of it is full of chemicals, and if you're happy in yourself, you don't need a drink to relax. I still have an occasional drink but I find that I want just a very small glass of wine or something diluted.

26 try alternative remedies

I cannot take antibiotics because of my earlier illness and I react pretty badly to most pharmaceuticals. Over the years, I have found alternative remedies, proper diet, and supplements to be extremely effective. I almost never get sick and if I do, I recover quickly. I once cured myself of an infection of the pleura with my soup (see page 76,) daily reflexology, and loads of vitamin C. Of course, you should always check with a doctor to ensure that you really do know what's wrong with you, and be aware of any complications you need to look out for.

Find the form of alternative medicine that suits you best, and a fully qualified practitioner with whom you can work on a regular basis to keep your body healthy. Alternative medicine focuses on treating the body holistically, understanding your own body chemistry, and knowing what works for you. The difference with alternative medicine is that you don't wait until you are ill to see someone. You work to keep your body in the best possible health, so that you do not become sick at all.

27 the importance of vitamin D

Everyone needs sun on their body

Everyone needs sun on their body. You cannot get enough vitamin D for your bones and general wellbeing without sun. Vitamin D3 is now known to be essential to the proper development and maintenance of healthy bones, and children who spend much of their time indoors run the risk of being deficient in this vital nutrient. Make sure that you go outside enough—even in winter. Just being outside ensures that some of those rays are touching you, although depending on where you live, the strength of the sun may be too weak to provide vitamin D. Take a vitamin D3 supplement in winter. If you work in an office, make the effort to go out at lunchtime and get some fresh air and light on your body—even if it's raining! You must not stay cooped up all day.

_28_ cut down on your sugar

We all need treats—just don't make yours a doughnut! Sugar is bad for you and refined sugar is the worst. Learn to love bars of 85% dark chocolate, check labels to find natural foods with less sugar, eat fresh fruit with plain yogurt sprinkled with nuts and seeds, use honey or agave syrup on yogurt or porridge. Keep non-sugary snacks in your bag, briefcase, or car. A magic thing happens when you cut down on sugar—you lose the taste for it. I always have some nuts or a bar of my favorite chocolate with me. I also take my own snacks if I'm traveling by air or train, so that I know what I'm eating.

29 retrain your taste buds

After a little while, you will find that you are no longer craving those foods that you have been avoiding

Once you have identified foods that don't suit you, be ruthless in cutting them out. Rather than feel that you're missing out, think of them as foods that harm you. Keep to those foods that do suit. After a little while, you may find that you dislike those foods that you have been avoiding when you try them again.

I used to love milky cappuccinos with lots of chocolate on top. They were one of my favorite treats. However, I realized that they probably weren't doing me any good, so I stopped drinking them. After about six months, I had a terrible yearning for one and I thought it couldn't possibly do any harm just to have one. I settled down in one of my favorite cafés with a huge steaming, chocolatey cappuccino to savour the moment. After one sip, I felt a headache start and it tasted foul. Quite extraordinary! I have never wanted one again.

It's the same with sugar. I used to have a very sweet tooth but now I actively dislike anything too sweet and look for desserts that contain little or no sugar.

30 remove temptation

Ridding the place of refined sugar may have an all-round calming effect

While you're retraining your taste buds, it makes sense to remove temptation. If you have only food that's good for you in the house, then that's what you'll eat. I realize it's much harder if you're feeding other people, but your husband/children/guests will also benefit from healthy food.

You may find that eating purer food, and more fruit and vegetables, affects the atmosphere of your household. Plenty of scientific evidence exists to show that refined sugar affects mood swings. Indeed, a recent study in California suggested that refined sugar should come with a health warning as grave as that associated with cigarettes.

ideas for healthy snacks:

❋ Houmous with raw carrots or celery. Carrots are a lovely sweet vegetable and delicious raw. I have them mid morning or afternoon if I feel like a quick bite.

❋ Gluten-free crackers with houmous and a great dollop of fresh parsley—parsley is very tasty and also provides masses of natural calcium for healthy bones and teeth.

❋ Organic nuts—almonds, brazils, and hazelnuts are particularly good, but not too much salt please.

❋ Canned sardines—hugely nutritious and great on a piece of gluten/yeast-free toast with a squeeze of lemon and a handful of parsley, or in a stir-fry.

❋ Toast—preferably wheat/yeast-free—with butter and nut butter. Nut butter is another great snack because it gives you some protein. It comes in a jar and is available in some supermarkets and health-food stores.

❋ Herbal teas—drink plenty because they help to suppress your appetite.

❋ Have a cook-up—make those casseroles and soups and freeze them so you've always got something yummy to eat.

❋ Keep fresh fruit in the fridge so it's always there but doesn't spoil.

31 stick to your ideal weight

When you eat properly and choose foods that suit you,
your weight will find its own natural level

Not everyone should be skinny. We all have a weight that suits us. Once you
know what yours is, try to stick to it. If your jeans are suddenly too tight, they're
too tight! Don't buy bigger ones. As model Kate Moss says, "Nothing tastes as
good as skinny feels." Although not too skinny! Nothing makes you feel better
about yourself than slipping into a dress and knowing that it flows over your
hips and stomach rather than strains to contain them.

All sorts of guidance is available on how much you should weigh. You can, of
course, consult a BMI (Body Mass Index) chart to show you where your weight
should be. This, however, is a broad spectrum. It doesn't take into account
whether you have small or large bones or whether your bones are light or
heavy. Everyone's frame is different. I am over 5 feet 9 inches tall so theoretically
could weigh at least 140lb and still be considered very healthy. The truth is
I would feel dreadful. I have tiny, light bones and am usually around
the 126lb mark.

If you never stray too far from your ideal weight, it's very easy to adjust it after an occasional lapse. I weigh myself every day in the morning. If I'm a pound or two up, I make sure that I'm back to normal by the next day. The extra pound may be a sign that I've eaten something that didn't agree with me and my body is therefore retaining fluid to compensate.

A pound or two is no big deal, but if I let my weight go up by five or six pounds, that's much harder to lose. Also it becomes easier for me to convince myself that it doesn't matter, when actually it does. I am exactly the same size as I have always been, and that means I can still wear some of the classic items of clothing that I've bought over the past 30 years. How's that for an added advantage!

32 find foods that suit you

If it doesn't suit you, don't eat it

One of the tricks of keeping your weight stable is identifying those foods that don't suit you. Everybody's body chemistry is different. We don't all suit the same foods any more than we suit the same clothes. The problem is that most people don't know what suits them. If you constantly eat food that isn't right for you, you may have low energy, bags under the eyes, a bloated stomach, headaches, or any number of minor symptoms, and you are probably constantly

battling your weight. For example, I can't eat potatoes. I don't know why but they make me constipated and blow up my stomach. So I just don't eat them. I can't eat cheese or drink coffee, either, but I can eat bars of 85% organic dark chocolate!

Foods that are most likely to cause intolerances include sugar, wheat, gluten, yeast, milk, cheese, and vegetables from the *Solanaceae* family: eggplants, peppers, and potatoes. I suggest cutting out all those for at least a month and then adding a small amount at one meal to see how you feel afterward. If you feel all right, try a small amount again but be careful not to overload the system, and watch for any reaction. Once the detox period is over, test one of them at a time over a couple of days, so that you are clear what works for you and what doesn't.

Keep a food diary for a month and note what you eat and how you feel afterward, including mood swings, bloating, heat flushes, or headaches. You can, of course, have tests to see what your sensitivities are. I find Kinesiology (muscle testing) works for me, but you can pretty much work it out for yourself.

33 drink lots of fluid

Keep your body really well hydrated and clear of toxins

This is so important. Your body needs plenty of liquid intake and that does not mean tea and coffee! Regular tea and coffee, and even decaffeinated coffee, do not count as the sort of fluid you need to keep your body really well hydrated and clear of toxins. The minute you add milk, or if any additive is present, the cleansing effect is taken away.

Water and herbal teas are the answer. So many amazing herbal teas are available, you are bound to find several that you really like. Try to drink at least four pints (a couple of litres) of fluid per day but be warned—tail off your liquid intake a couple of hours before bedtime. You don't want to be visiting the bathroom all night or have puffy eyes in the morning.

I always start the day with a mug of boiling water containing a good chunk of fresh ginger and a few slices of lemon. That helps to clean the system before having breakfast.

There is nothing wrong with having an occasional cup of regular tea or coffee if your body doesn't react to it, but don't count these toward your overall fluid intake during the day, and please keep them organic.

34 don't get constipated

Start the day with an infusion of fresh ginger and lemon

If your food is not being digested properly, something is wrong. Either you are eating foods that don't suit you or you are eating too quickly. Assuming you have no medical reason for constipation, changing your diet, drinking plenty of fluid, and eating more slowly should solve the problem.

Try to eat a high-fibre breakfast. I make up mine with a variety of gluten-free cereals, adding nuts, seeds, and fruit, and I have it with rice, almond, or soya milk. I also start the day with an infusion of fresh ginger and lemon which helps clear the system. After breakfast, I find that eating fewer carbs helps. The idea is to keep your system clean and free of toxins. It is always a good idea to use golden linsuit on a daily basis. Mix one tablespoon of linsuit with about the same quantity or slightly more of boiled water and leave it to stand. Mix into your cereal, porridge, smoothie, or yogurt.

It is a good idea to have fresh mint or camomile tea after a meal, or any of the herbal teas aimed at helping digestion. I keep supplements recommended by my nutritionist for when I've eaten out and had something that didn't quite agree with me to ensure I stay regular. Ideally, you should go after each meal and at least once a day. It shows the digestive system is functioning perfectly.

35 keep fit

We have talked about yoga and walking, my own preferred methods of staying trim. However, many people like more activity, and obviously taking part in sports and spending time in the gym can be of great benefit. As with food, every body is different and requires differing levels of exercise to maintain optimum health. Your heart and bones in particular need regular exercise. I would just add a word of caution—jogging can seriously damage your knees and joints over time, so be careful to have plenty of omega oils, for instance by including oily fish in your diet. Seeds such as linseed and sunflower are very good, too, as are oily dressings on your salads, and a plant-based oil supplement will give you additional omega oil. Remember that if you overdevelop muscles, you will always need to keep them at a certain level or they will go flabby. Swimming is an excellent overall exercise as are walking and dancing.

36 cook (and waste) less food
Don't waste anything

If you want to stay fit and healthy, you shouldn't eat too much. Endless studies show that people who have lower calorific intakes with diets rich in oils, fruit, and vegetables are healthier. If you are eating foods that suit you (see page 66), your body absorbs nutrients more easily. I find that if I stick to a diet that works for me, I do not have hunger cravings, but if I eat food that does not suit me, I want more—perhaps my body is telling me that it didn't get enough goodness.

Don't waste anything. To me, it is entirely wrong to waste food, and particularly any part of an animal, bird or fish that gave its life so that humans could eat it. So I make sure that every part of what I buy is eaten. For example, if I buy a chicken or pheasant, I roast it, use every part of it, and then turn the bones into homemade stock. Nothing takes long to do. It's just a question of habit. I buy much less than I used to and anything left over ends up in soup.

I live on my own so it's easy to cook more food than I need— in fact, it's quite hard not to. I make a lot of casseroles and soups, which I divide into small portions and freeze. I find that an old 1lb (450g) yogurt or soup carton is just the right size for freezing individual portions. One of those thawed gives me two meals. I am also a great stir-fryer! Any left-over veggies, meat, or fish can go in the wok with some Braggs Liquid Aminos (an excellent soya sauce substitute) and sometimes a dash of sweet chili sauce. I always have leeks and pumpkin seeds to add, which seem to make everything taste good. Even fruit can be added to a stir-fry. Papaya or mango are delicious when stirred in right at the end. Use toasted sesame oil or coconut oil for stir-frying—it tastes great and is particularly suited to that type of cooking.

Cook less, eat a bit less, and don't waste anything. Your stomach will shrink and you will wonder how on earth you used to eat so much.

37 eat slowly

Food is precious, so savor each mouthful

Eating slowly is advice often given and just as often ignored. The slower you eat, the more time your stomach has to register that it is full. Drink a glass of water before you start, because it helps to suppress the appetite. Think about how it was produced and the effort that went into preparing it.

Follow these tips …

✳ Chew each mouthful properly, don't bolt your food.

✳ Make time to eat. I always have a lunch break so that I can relax as well as eat.

✳ If you are eating with family or friends, enjoy the company and talk between mouthfuls so that your body has time to register the food you've eaten. Mealtimes should be special whether you are on your own or with others.

✳ Drink tea with your meal—the Chinese and Japanese have always benefited from drinking green tea with their meals.

✳ Make sure your back is straight while you eat. If your stomach is cramped, your digestion will suffer and you may have stomach ache afterward.

✳ If you are eating food that suits you, slowly, you won't feel hungry an hour after you've eaten; nor will you crave sugary snacks.

38 read labels

I am an inveterate label reader. If there are too many ingredients (particularly ones that you don't instantly recognize,) you probably don't want to eat it. The best food is fresh and pure. To start with, reading labels is very boring but you will soon realize just how many chemicals and assorted additives you've been putting in your body. Read labels on vitamins and supplements, too. Not all of them are pure. My mother has osteoarthritis, so I had my bone density checked, and my doctor recommended that I take a daily calcium supplement. I duly took my prescription to my local chemist but when I read the label on the tablets, I saw that they contained aspartame, an artificial sweetener. All sorts of theories have been put forward about aspartame, but I would never knowingly ingest it, and certainly not every day.

39 dealing with colds and minor infections

Please don't go to your doctor demanding antibiotics for coughs, colds, or any minor viral infection. Check that you don't have anything other than an ordinary virus by all means, and then treat it yourself.

The minute I notice that scratchy feeling in the throat, I make a huge pot of soup. Use your homemade stock, or otherwise a yeast-free one. Put in lots of organic vegetables—onions, parsnips, leeks, carrots, loads of garlic, and lentils— and cook on a low heat in a covered pan for a couple of hours to seal in the goodness. Stay off everything else. If you need a bit of bulk with it, have some yeast- and gluten-free toasted bread to dunk, or gluten-free crackers with organic, unsalted butter. Have your soup every couple of hours, or as often as you want. I promise you it clears the system and you will feel better.

Your soup will provide lots of natural vitamin C but do take a vitamin C supplement as well. You can also eat fresh fruit so long as you don't put anything on it, and you should drink plenty of fluids. These should be herb teas or hot water with fresh ginger and lemon (try putting grated ginger and a piece of lemon into green tea—it's delicious.) You can add Manuka honey to any drink— it has a natural antibiotic quality that will help sore throats. While you have any

kind of viral infection, keep off all dairy products except organic unsalted butter. Don't even have a drop of milk in tea. Don't eat carbs apart from the odd piece of toast or cracker. Just clean the body and boost your natural immune system so it can do its job for you.

40 get plenty of sleep

Very few things make you look and feel better than a good night's sleep

Everyone needs sleep to stay fit and healthy and yet a huge percentage of us go through periods when we have difficulty in achieving those six to eight hours of shuteye. My last drink of the day is always a herbal tea with valerian or other sleep-inducing herbs, but many natural remedies are available for those who are having trouble sleeping. However, any kind of insomnia usually has an underlying cause. So if you have regular problems, talk to your doctor and then check out alternative therapies, such as massage, acupuncture, color light therapy, and NLP (neurolinguistic programing.) Try to establish what's preventing you from sleeping. Is it stress, diet, or maybe subconscious memories? A friend of mine's house was once burgled while she was asleep, and her subconscious was stopping her from achieving deep sleep. A session of NLP helped her enormously.

PART 3

Mind & Spirit

So much of looking good comes from how we feel inside. We all know that if you start the day feeling good and with a smile on your face, the chances are that the rest of the day will progress well. Somehow people are friendlier and work flows better. Equally, a grumpy beginning often leads to crossness at small irritations and nothing being quite right all day. One of the most important lessons I have learned is not to be fixated on just one goal but to look at the whole picture and be ready to change your approach to any given situation, no matter what.

41 the power of the universe

Everything that happens gives us a chance to re-evaluate

No matter how hard you plan or how well you have prepared, sometimes things just don't go the way you want them to. If volcanic ash grounds planes, or a tsunami hits your business destination, or if the highway is closed because of a fire, there is absolutely nothing that you can do about it. Equally, but in much smaller ways, our best-laid plans are occasionally thwarted through absolutely no fault of our own. Rather than rail against fate, I always look to see what new opportunity has arisen because of the unexpected changes. I try to take the view that there is a reason for it—I do not believe in coincidences.

Everything that happens gives us a chance to re-evaluate what we are doing, meet new people, do something else, or even just gives us a break in our day. If you view every event as an opportunity for a new or better experience, you will be less stressed and more open to exciting new possibilities.

42 breathe properly

Try to make deep breathing a habit

If you are stressed, panicked, or unhappy, you can usually feel yourself breathing in the top part of your chest. Take a moment to notice your breathing. Then consciously breathe from the lower part of your abdomen. Slow down your breathing and see how quickly you start to calm down. Try to make deep breathing a habit. Be aware of your own breath and take time in your day to adjust it. If you're having an argument or feeling emotional, literally take a few deep breaths—remove yourself from the situation to somewhere a bit quieter and breathe deeply. It really works!

a simple breathing exercise:

✳ Place the first and second fingers of your right hand on your forehead, the third and fourth fingers lightly on your left nostril and your thumb on your right nostril. Exhale to the count of five.

✳ Close the right nostril with your thumb and inhale deeply through the left nostril to the count of five.

✳ Close both nostrils, holding your breath for a count of five.

✳ Exhale slowly through the right nostril for a count of five.

✳ Release both nostrils but stay without breath for a count of five and then repeat in reverse.

✳ Repeat four times.

✳ Now here's the important bit. As you exhale, let go of whatever is troubling you or any anger or negatives. When you inhale, breathe in what you most desire—love, joy, abundance, or whatever is most important to you. Hold your positive thought as you hold your breath and then breathe out the negatives again.

✳ You are breathing out what you don't want in your life and breathing in what you do. It's remarkably effective.

43 quiet time

Meditation is a way of giving yourself quiet time

Most people think that meditation means being able to miraculously transport themselves to a blissful place in the ether. This may be true for some but not many. It is amazing how we all profess to be unable to take 10 or 15 minutes out of our day just to be peaceful, and yet we are unlikely to say we don't have time to browse the internet or watch TV. When I first started meditation, I could barely sit still for 10 minutes. Now I find that 20 or even 30 pass by, leaving me relaxed and calm. Often, solutions to problems occur to me after meditating.

Meditation or quiet time is food for the soul, and if you feed your soul, the more at ease you are likely to be. Plenty of advice on meditation techniques is available, but here's a simple way to start:

✳ Find somewhere quiet and sit on a chair with a straight back, or one that has lots of cushions to support your back.

✳ If you have a meditation tape, play it quietly in the background.

✳ Sit on your chair, back straight, but make sure you are comfortable.

✳ Gently place you right ankle over your left and relax your hands in your lap, your right hand gently resting in your left palm, or place your thumbs and forefingers together.

✳ Count up to 60 and just imagine light pouring into your body.

✳ Count all your blessings in life and ask your God or the universe for guidance in whichever part of your life you feel needs assistance.

✳ Don't try to blank your mind, but rather accept that a cacophony of thoughts are swirling around your head. Be aware of them, almost like an outsider watching them. (Explore this idea in *The Power of Now*, Eckhart Tolle's illuminating book.) Now concentrate on the light flooding through your body and let peace wash over you.

✳ When you are ready, count down from 60, then gently resume your day or evening.

44 always be positive

There is a reason for everything we experience

There is absolutely no point in always seeing the dark side of a situation. That does not mean being unrealistic—what it does mean is looking for the positive. No matter how black things may seem, some form of compensation is usually to be found somewhere, and remember, every new situation opens another door. You will feel happier if you are looking for positives. Just being positive may help you to react better with other people, which in turn tends to lead to better outcomes.

For example, after a very close friend of mine got divorced, she had her heart set on a little house with a garden for her and her two boys. Yet three times the sale fell through. I told her that it obviously wasn't "her house" and something better for her would come along. It did, and quite out of the blue. She found a flat that had a door onto a huge communal garden, which gave the boys somewhere much better to play. She has been grateful that she didn't buy the little house ever since.

If I am stuck in a traffic jam or on a train, I try to focus on something beautiful that I can see, even if it's just a single flower growing in a built-up environment. Otherwise, I mull over what it is the extra time has given me space to think

about. Is there something I haven't noticed? The universe has just slowed me down so there must be a reason.

If you go for a job interview and don't succeed in your application, think about what you learned from the interview. That was someone else's job. Something better for you will come along. Is it time to think about doing something quite different? Did you meet someone else on the way who may lead to another opening or a new friendship?

I believe with all my heart that there is a reason for everything we experience and for us being wherever we find ourselves. Sometimes we go through very difficult times but what we learn during that period makes us stronger and it guides us to a happier and more fulfilling life.

45 let go of bitterness

Bitterness held inside shows on the outside

Yes, I know the sayings: don't get mad, get even, and an eye for an eye. None of us likes unfairness or injustice. We rail against it and seek to rectify whatever we perceive as life dealing a nasty blow. All I can tell you is bitterness held inside shows on the outside. I am also convinced it leads to poor health and illness. You have to deal with what you can and be prepared just to let go of the rest. Of course, if someone betrays you in a personal or business capacity, you won't want to have anything to do with that person again. If you can't avoid the person, it can be tough, but you don't have to trust him or her—and don't let it eat away at you. Your face will tell the story and you'll have frown lines and wrinkles you don't deserve, not to mention poor digestion. Let the guilty party feel the guilt and strain—you just relax!

I do believe we reap what we sow, and life is too short to spend it trying to exact retribution on those who don't deserve our time or energy. Take some quiet time and let it go. You'll be amazed at how things have a way of sorting themselves out.

46 dance

My brother and I used to call people who were no good at dancing quimblers!
It doesn't matter whether you have rhythm or not. Put on your favorite music
and dance around your home! Few things lift the spirits more than a rock
around the kitchen, bedroom, or bathroom. Let it rip. It is very good exercise
and it's very hard to be depressed when you're bopping in the hallway.

47 try new things

It's so easy to say we don't like things when in fact we haven't tried them. Whether it's food, a different sport, exhibitions, a new place, or hobby, just give it a go. Try to make a point of doing something different at least once a month. When a colleague suggests a different place to go at lunchtime, or a friend wants you to join her at a class, or one of your family wants you to watch a different sport with him, try it. After all, if you really don't like it, you don't have to do it again, but opening up your horizons is an important part of staying young.

48 candles, incense, and a tidy space

Declutter regularly

Creating a peaceful environment in your home is one of the most important ways to stay calm and to ensure stress doesn't stay with you for any length of time. If your home is very untidy, it is hard to relax. Declutter regularly and organize all your things. I can find places to install cupboards that no one ever thought of! A tidy home helps keep a happy mind. When everything is tidy, you can create the right atmosphere. Nowadays, scented candles and incense are readily available, and different aromas can be used to relax, invigorate, or set a theme, such as Christmas. Choose whatever suits your mood and the occasion, and let the lovely smells waft around your home. Just don't leave candles unattended! Burning the house down is not good for your stress levels!

49 "me" space and time

No matter how busy you are, how many friends you have, or the size of your family, you need your own space. "Me" time is essential. We have talked about quiet time and to have that, you need to create "me" space. Choose your bedroom or bathroom or any other room where you can close the door and put a "Do Not Disturb" sign on it. Make sure everyone knows that they absolutely cannot come in while you're having your "me" time. It may be that you make it around bathtime or at a particular time of day, but in that place at that time, you should be left alone. Light your candles or incense, meditate, or just do your nails, but have time for yourself in an uncluttered space.

50 the power of pets
Animals give unconditional love

Little soothes the senses as much as a beloved pet. Indeed, the benefits of pet ownership are well documented. Some hospitals, hospices, and retirement homes encourage visitors to bring their pets with them. Of course, you have to be sure that you have time to look after your pet properly, whatever it is, and even if it's very small. I rescued two cats from Celia Hammond's refuge in Canning Town, London. They are the lights of my life, always there to purr and comfort, help me watch my favorite programs, and cuddle up. Animals give unconditional love. They bring a different energy to the home and give so much more than they take. But they are a responsibility and you must think through how they will be looked after if you are away or out at the office or socializing a great deal. All animals need company and dislike being left for long periods, so be very sure you have a lifestyle that allows you to be with them, or consider sharing an animal. A great friend of mine and her neighbors adopted a stray cat in their area, sharing responsibility for its needs. Lady Alice, as she was called, became a much-loved communal pet and helped bring a part of the community together.

51 look at nature

Take time to appreciate nature

No matter what is going on in your life, take time to appreciate nature. Nothing is as beautiful as the first spring blossom or bluebells. Nature is stunning whether it's the song of a bird or the roar of the sea. Take time to appreciate it. If you live in a town, plant a window box, treat yourself to a few flowers, or walk in a local park. If you're in the country or by the sea, remember to appreciate everything around you. Even a couple of minutes spent focusing on nature calms the soul, and if you're walking, try to notice every tree, flower, and bird—it's almost as good as a mini vacation! If I'm stuck in a traffic jam, I always try to look at something beautiful to stop me feeling aggravated. It is amazing how even in very built-up areas, a lone flower or tree can raise the spirits.

52 enjoy hobbies

Try to learn different skills, or make yourself more knowledgeable

Take up pastimes that bring you pleasure, whether they enable you to meet new people or you pursue them on your own—and preferably a combination of both. You can do puzzles, read books, attend classes, watch sports, help charities, or volunteer for local organizations, but open up your mind to things outside your everyday life. Try to learn different skills, or make yourself more knowledgeable. It's important that some of your hobbies get you out of your usual environment. Just seeing new places or buildings adds to your life and opens up new possibilities.

53 smile and laugh

Laughter is proven to have a beneficial effect on the body and mind

Go to a mirror now and smile! Just doing it makes you feel better. At the risk of having people think you are marginally strange, smile at them. It is amazing how infectious smiling can be. Smiling eases tension and sets you off on the right foot with anyone you are meeting. Most find it quite hard not to smile back and then you both feel good.

Laughter is proven to have a beneficial effect on the body and mind. Watch your favorite comedy programs on TV, spend time with friends or family who make you laugh, read something funny, but make sure you have lots of laughter in your life. Most situations in life have a funny side. Try to find it. A stonking good laugh is one of nature's best medicines.

54 appreciate your family
Don't dwell on perceived slights or disagreements

Value the shared history that you have within your family. Some of us are very close to our families, others not so much, but however you feel, there is a bond that cannot be replicated elsewhere. See the positives in the relationships and value the different generations. Don't dwell on perceived slights or disagreements. They are your family and probably see you differently from the way your friends see you. Something about growing up together tends to give siblings or other close relatives a firm view of how you are, which is often miles away from how your friends know you. Don't let it bother you—just love and appreciate them as individuals and make the most of time spent together.

55 nurture your friendships

To have good friends is to be truly blessed. I think that I have the best friends in the world and could never have got through some of the very difficult times in my life without them. Nurture your friendships. Understand their value. Be thoughtful to your friends; imagine what you would like to hear if you were in their place. Listen to their problems as much as they listen to yours. Love and cherish them. Don't hold grudges, talk through any disagreements, and keep in touch with them if they move away. Good friends are much less expensive and more fun than psychoanalysis. Very often shared experiences put a different perspective on whatever is happening in your life and the old adage of a problem shared being a problem halved is almost certainly true.

56 love the seasons

Every season has something to be excited about

Love every season. Spring is magical as nature wakes from winter. Summer brings long days and warm weather with time to spend in parks and gardens. Fall gives us stunning colors and the vibrant scents of bonfires as well as all the activity leading up to Christmas. Winter brings chestnuts to roast, a chance to nestle in the warmth of our homes, and Christmas to spend with friends and relatives. Staying young means finding the positives in everything around you and looking forward to something special in every part of the year.

57 love yourself

You are unique and special

You can't expect anyone else to love you if you don't love yourself. Feeling good about yourself gives an inner confidence that shows in everything you do and how you look. Write down all your good points and remind yourself of them when your confidence flags or you've had a knock at the office or in your love life. Don't let yourself be badly treated by others. Respect yourself and others will respect you, too.

58 develop spiritual practice

We've talked about meditation and having quiet time. It doesn't matter what religion you were brought up in, which one you choose, or whether you prefer to communicate with the universe without ritual. What matters is that you believe in an all-powerful goodness you can talk to and from whom you can seek guidance. A quiet church is the most wonderful place to find calm in a storm, hymns are amazingly uplifting, praying to any God helps settle the soul. Feel connected to everything that is light and love. It will radiate through you in all that you do and give you comfort when you most need it.

59 read

Enjoy the beauty of words

Whatever your likes and dislikes, adding to your knowledge is a good thing. Read the classics, poetry, whodunits set in interesting places, biographies, history, and anything else that grabs your attention, but keep your mind open. Enjoy the beauty of words and explore different views and cultures. Feeling young at heart comes in part from having an open and inquisitive mind, and in these days of ipads and Kindles, the world is one giant library.

60 help others

There's nothing quite like helping someone else to make you understand how blessed you are. Smile at the elderly, let them know that they are not unnoticed. Help a young mum with a pram; volunteer for a charity or at a local school or project. My favorite grandmother was always rushing off to take some "old lady" to the doctors or chiropodist even though the old lady was often younger than she was! Even little things mean a lot and somehow helping someone else always makes you feel better and more alive.

Good luck!

So that's it—my 60 ways to help you improve your wellbeing. Look after your body and your health, of course, but you cannot stay young unless your spirit is strong. Take the positives from every part of your life. As you mature, enjoy the confidence that comes with it, the self-knowledge, and the satisfaction of having got thus far with a modicum of success. Stay young by keeping the mind active and alive. Try new things but remember to value the old. Stay balanced and wise. Life is wonderful. Live every minute as it happens and enjoy every moment.

My personal notebook

LOTIONS, POTIONS & FACIALS

Essential Care: Organic creams and treatments for the whole family, handmade in Suffolk, England. Not a dodgy ingredient in sight and seriously environmentally friendly.
www.essential-care.co.uk

Katherine Jackson: Plumps up the skin with a hi-tech laser machine used in conjunction with her own all-natural serum. Some products are available online. Katherine also does terrific massages, reflexology, and regular facials. www.katherinejackson.co.uk

Merrywood: Handmade natural products, not tested on animals. Range includes beautiful-to-look-at and delicious-smelling soaps, candles, botanicals, and oils.
www.merrywood.co.uk

Neal's Yard Remedies: Possibly my favorite high-street brand. Superb products made from all-natural ingredients. They also do excellent facials and massages.
www.nealsyardremedies.com

Pure Lochside: Range of organic skincare made from high-quality ingredients.
www.purelochside.com

HERBALISTS

Susan Koten MNIMH, MRCHM/ Willow Herbal Centre: Sue rescued me from the *giardia* stomach bug among other things. Her comfrey ointment is brilliant for skin rashes and her throat spray a lifesaver if you feel a cold coming on.
www.willowherbalcentre.co.uk

Register of Chinese Herbal Medicine:
www.rchm.co.uk

National Institute of Medical Herbalists (NIMH):
www.nimh.org.uk

HAIR

Label M Organics, by Toni & Guy: Offers a range of organic haircare products
www.labelm.com

Toni & Guy: This is where I go for my Brazilian blow-dry. One of the best hairdressers, they now have salons worldwide, plus a fantastic range of organic products.
www.toniandguy.com

NUTRITIONAL ADVICE

Jackie Hales/Larkfield Complementary Health Centre: Jackie was an ME sufferer and finally found a way to make herself better. She uses the BEST system and has had amazing results with all kinds of eating and fatigue-related problems.

Maria Candida De Melo: My favorite nutritionist, affiliated to the British Association for Nutritional Therapy (BANT)—a bit of a taskmaster but oh so good!
www.individualnutritionaltherapy.com

British Nutrition Foundation:
www.nutrition.org.uk/

TEA

Tea Palace: My favorite teas come from here—including white peony and rosebud. They have over 120 black, oolong, green, white, and flowering teas, plus an exclusive selection of Tea Tonics—organic herbal infusions specifically blended to improve wellbeing according to Ayurvedic remedies.
http://www.teapalace.co.uk

YOGA:

Gemma McCoy is a friend and yoga muse. If you are just starting out with yoga, there is no one better.
www.gemmamccoy.com

RECOMMENDED READING

The Power of Now, Eckhart Tolle—a must read for those who enjoyed the spiritual part of my book.

500 of the Most Important Health Tips You'll Ever Need, Hazel Courteney—my personal guide that I use all the time when I need advice on health and supplements. No home should be without a copy!

SPAS

Cameron House Hotel, Scotland:
www.cameronhouse.co.uk
The Carlisle Bay Hotel, Antigua:
www.elegantresorts.co.uk
The Four Seasons, Mahe, Seychelles:
www.fourseasons.com/seychelles/spa
Kempinski Hotel, Bodrum, Turkey:
www.classic-collection.co.uk
The Marbella Club, Spain:
www.marbellaclub.com
The Merrion, Dublin:
www.merrionhotel.com
Park Hyatt, Istanbul, Turkey:
Istanbul.park.hyatt.com
Raffles Praslin, Seychelles:
www.raffles.com/praslin
The Riad Al Ksar, Marrakesh, Morocco:
www.alksar.com/eng/
Runnymede Hotel, England:
www.runnymedehotel.co.uk
St Pancras Spa, London:
www.stpancrasspa.co.uk

Index

Acknowledgments

Having a first book published is a very special experience. This one would never have happened without the advice and support of several of my wonderful friends. So huge thanks go to Rowan Pelling for her incredibly generous introduction, to Gemma McCoy for helping make sure my yoga exercises looked right in the photographs, and to Mandy Tucker for styling my hair. To Hazel Courteney for her unceasing kindness, support, and introductions, to Cristina Odone and Liz Hunt for encouraging me to write and giving me the opportunity, and to Linda Joyce who helped me define the type of book this should be. I am blessed with amazing friends and my thanks go to all of them for always being there for me. Last but not least I am indebted to Cindy Richards, Dawn Bates, Clare Sayer, and the Cico team for making my first publishing experience so enjoyable.

Picture Credits
© **Shutterstock:** 2, 106; **Emma Mitchell:** 3, 7, 10, 14, 21, 23, 53, 59, 60, 66, 69, 75, 84, 87, 98, 101, 105, 107; **Nicki Dowey:** 5 left; **David Montgomery:** 5 right, 43, 54; **Dan Duchars:** 17, 34, 79; © **istock photography:** 18, 25, 39, 45, 48, 50, 80, 83, 91, 95; **Daniel Farmer:** 29, 31, 33; **Lisa Linder:** 41; **Stuart West:** 27, 30; **Tino Tedaldi:** 37, 47; **Gavin Kingcombe:** 57; **Gloria Nicol:** 62, 72; **Mark Scott:** 65; **Winfried Heinze:** 71, 77; **David Brittain:** 86; **Melanie Eclare:** 89; **Christopher Drake:** 93; **Debi Treloar:** 96; **Jonathan Gregson:** 97;